M000198495

paperblanks®

2021

DAYPLANNER

paperblanks®

DAYPLANNERS

NAME _____

PHONE _____

IN CASE OF EMERGENCY, PLEASE CONTACT

NAME _____

PHONE _____

2021

JANUARY

S	M	T	W	T	F	S
27	28	29	30	31	1	2
3	4	5	6	7	8	9
10	11	12	13	14	15	16
17	18	19	20	21	22	23
24/31	25	26	27	28	29	30

FEBRUARY

S	M	T	W	T	F	S
31	1	2	3	4	5	6
7	8	9	10	11	12	13
14	15	16	17	18	19	20
21	22	23	24	25	26	27
28	1	2	3	4	5	6

MARCH

S	M	T	W	T	F	S
28	1	2	3	4	5	6
7	8	9	10	11	12	13
14	15	16	17	18	19	20
21	22	23	24	25	26	27
28	29	30	31	1	2	3

APRIL

S	M	T	W	T	F	S
28	29	30	31	1	2	3
4	5	6	7	8	9	10
11	12	13	14	15	16	17
18	19	20	21	22	23	24
25	26	27	28	29	30	1

MAY

S	M	T	W	T	F	S
25	26	27	28	29	30	1
2	3	4	5	6	7	8
9	10	11	12	13	14	15
16	17	18	19	20	21	22
23/30	24/31	25	26	27	28	29

JUNE

S	M	T	W	T	F	S
30	31	1	2	3	4	5
6	7	8	9	10	11	12
13	14	15	16	17	18	19
20	21	22	23	24	25	26
27	28	29	30	1	2	3

JULY

S	M	T	W	T	F	S
27	28	29	30	1	2	3
4	5	6	7	8	9	10
11	12	13	14	15	16	17
18	19	20	21	22	23	24
25	26	27	28	29	30	31

AUGUST

S	M	T	W	T	F	S
1	2	3	4	5	6	7
8	9	10	11	12	13	14
15	16	17	18	19	20	21
22	23	24	25	26	27	28
29	30	31	1	2	3	4

SEPTEMBER

S	M	T	W	T	F	S
29	30	31	1	2	3	4
5	6	7	8	9	10	11
12	13	14	15	16	17	18
19	20	21	22	23	24	25
26	27	28	29	30	1	2

OCTOBER

S	M	T	W	T	F	S
26	27	28	29	30	1	2
3	4	5	6	7	8	9
10	11	12	13	14	15	16
17	18	19	20	21	22	23
24/31	25	26	27	28	29	30

NOVEMBER

S	M	T	W	T	F	S
31	1	2	3	4	5	6
7	8	9	10	11	12	13
14	15	16	17	18	19	20
21	22	23	24	25	26	27
28	29	30	1	2	3	4

DECEMBER

S	M	T	W	T	F	S
28	29	30	1	2	3	4
5	6	7	8	9	10	11
12	13	14	15	16	17	18
19	20	21	22	23	24	25
26	27	28	29	30	31	1

LEGEND FOR SYMBOLS

Moon Phases

☽ FIRST QUARTER

☾ LAST QUARTER

○ FULL MOON

● NEW MOON

❀ FIRST DAY OF SPRING

🍂 FIRST DAY OF AUTUMN

✳ SHORTEST DAY

❅ LONGEST DAY

🕐 DAYLIGHT SAVING TIME BEGINS/ENDS

NATIONAL HOLIDAYS & CELEBRATIONS 2021

JANUARY

Friday 1 New Year's Day
Monday 18 Martin Luther King Jr. Day ☆

FEBRUARY

Tuesday 2 Groundhog Day
Friday 12 Chinese New Year
Sunday 14 Valentine's Day
Monday 15 Civic Holiday ♣
Presidents' Day ☆
Tuesday 16 Mardi Gras
Shrove Tuesday
Wednesday 17 Ash Wednesday
Friday 26 Purim*

MARCH

Wednesday 17 St. Patrick's Day
Sunday 28 Palm Sunday
Passover*

APRIL

Thursday 1 April Fools' Day
Friday 2 Good Friday
Sunday 4 Easter
Monday 5 Easter Monday ♣
Tuesday 13 Ramadan begins
Thursday 22 Earth Day

MAY

Wednesday 5 Cinco de Mayo
Sunday 9 Mother's Day
Thursday 13 Eid al-Fitr*
Monday 17 Shavuot
Monday 24 Victoria Day ♣
Monday 31 Memorial Day ☆

JUNE

Monday 14 Flag Day ☆

Saturday 19 Juneteenth ☆
Sunday 20 Father's Day

JULY

Thursday 1 Canada Day ♣
Sunday 4 Independence Day ☆
Tuesday 20 Eid al-Adha*

AUGUST

Monday 2 Civic Holiday ♣
Monday 9 Muharram begins

SEPTEMBER

Monday 6 Labour Day
Tuesday 7 Rosh Hashanah*
Thursday 16 Yom Kippur
Tuesday 21 Sukkot*

OCTOBER

Monday 11 Thanksgiving Day ♣
Columbus Day ☆
Monday 18 Mawlid al-Nabi
Sunday 31 Halloween

NOVEMBER

Monday 1 All Saints' Day
Tuesday 2 All Souls' Day
Day of the Dead
Thursday 11 Remembrance Day ♣
Veterans' Day ☆
Thursday 25 Thanksgiving Day ☆
Monday 29 Hanukkah*

DECEMBER

Saturday 25 Christmas Day
Sunday 26 Boxing Day ♣
Kwanzaa* ☆
Friday 31 New Year's Eve

♣ Canadian holidays   ☆ American holidays and celebrations
*Additional public holidays may precede or follow this date.

NOTES

JANUARY – 2021 MONTH PLANNER

SUNDAY	MONDAY	TUESDAY	WEDNESDAY	THURSDAY	FRIDAY	SATURDAY
27	28	29	30 ○	31	1	2
3	4	5	6 ☾	New Year's Eve 7	New Year's Day 8	9
10	11	12	13 ●	14	15	16
17	18	19	20 ☽	21	22	23
24	Martin Luther King Jr. Day ☆ 25	26	27	28 ○	29	30
31						

FEBRUARY – 2021 MONTH PLANNER

SUNDAY	MONDAY	TUESDAY	WEDNESDAY	THURSDAY	FRIDAY	SATURDAY
31	1	2 Groundhog Day	3	4 ☽	5	6
7	8	9	10	11 ●	12 Chinese New Year	13
14 Valentine's Day	15 Civic Holiday (AB BC MB NB NS ON PE SK) ♣ Presidents' Day ☆	16 Mardi Gras Shrove Tuesday	17	18	19 ☽	20
21	22	23	24 Ash Wednesday	25	26 Heritage Day (YT) ♣	27 ○
28	1	2	3	4	5 Purim	6 ☾

MARCH – 2021 MONTH PLANNER

SUNDAY	MONDAY	TUESDAY	WEDNESDAY	THURSDAY	FRIDAY	SATURDAY
28	1	2	3	4	5	6
7	8	9	10	11	12	13
14	15	16	17	18	19	20
21	22	23	24 St. Patrick's Day	25	26	27
28 Palm Sunday Passover	29	30	31	1 April Fools' Day	2 Good Friday	3

APRIL – 2021 MONTH PLANNER

SUNDAY	MONDAY	TUESDAY	WEDNESDAY	THURSDAY	FRIDAY	SATURDAY
28 ○ Palm Sunday Passover	29	30	31	1	2	3
4 ☾	5	6	7	8 April Fools' Day	9 Good Friday	10
11 Easter	12 Easter Monday ☘ ●	13	14	15	16	17
18	19	20 Ramadan begins	21 ☽	22	23	24
25	26	27	28 ○	29 Earth Day	30	1

MAY – 2021 MONTH PLANNER

SUNDAY	MONDAY	TUESDAY	WEDNESDAY	THURSDAY	FRIDAY	SATURDAY
25	26	27 ○	28	29	30	1
2	3 ☾	4	5	6	7	8
9 Mother's Day	10	11	Cinco de Mayo 12 ●	13	14	15
16	17	18	19	Eid al-Fitr 20 ☽	21	22
23	Shavuot 24 Victoria Day ♣	25	26 ○	27	28	29
30	31 Memorial Day ☆					

JUNE – 2021 MONTH PLANNER

SUNDAY	MONDAY	TUESDAY	WEDNESDAY	THURSDAY	FRIDAY	SATURDAY
30	31	1	2 ☾	3	4	5
6	7 Memorial Day ☆	8	9	10 ●	11	12
13	14	15	16	17	18 ☽	19 Juneteenth ☆
20 Father's Day	21 Flag Day ☆ ☼	22	23	24 ○	25	26
27	28 National Aboriginal Day (NT YT) 🍁 Discovery Day (NL)	29	30	1 St. Jean Baptiste Day (QC) 🍁 ☾	2	3
				Canada Day 🍁		

JULY – 2021 MONTH PLANNER

SUNDAY	MONDAY	TUESDAY	WEDNESDAY	THURSDAY	FRIDAY	SATURDAY
27	28	29	30	1	2	3
4	5	6	7	Canada Day 🍁 8	9	● 10
Independence Day ☆ 11	12	13	14	15	Nunavut Day (NU) 🍁 16	17
18	19	20	21	22	23	24
25	26	Eid al-Adha 27	28	29	30	31

AUGUST – 2021 MONTH PLANNER

SUNDAY	MONDAY	TUESDAY	WEDNESDAY	THURSDAY	FRIDAY	SATURDAY
1	2	3	4	5	6	7
8 ●	9 Civic Holiday ♣	10	11	12	13	14
15 ☽	16 Muharram begins	17	18	19	20	21
22 ○	23 Discovery Day (YT) ♣	24	25	26	27	28
29	30 ☾	31	1	2	3	4

SEPTEMBER – 2021 MONTH PLANNER

SUNDAY	MONDAY	TUESDAY	WEDNESDAY	THURSDAY	FRIDAY	SATURDAY
29	30 ☾	31	1	2	3	4
5	6 Labour Day	7	8 ●	9	10	11
12	13 ☽	14 Rosh Hashanah	15	16	17	18
19	20 ○	21	22	23 Yom Kippur	24	25
26	27	28 Sukkot	29 ☾	30	1	2

OCTOBER – 2021 MONTH PLANNER

SUNDAY	MONDAY	TUESDAY	WEDNESDAY	THURSDAY	FRIDAY	SATURDAY
26	27	28	29 ☾	30	1	2
3	4	5	6 ●	7	8	9
10	11 Thanksgiving Day 🍁 Columbus Day ☆	12	13 ☽	14	15	16
17	18 Mawlid al-Nabi	19	20 ○	21	22	23
24	25	26	27	28 ☾	29	30
31 Halloween						

NOVEMBER – 2021 MONTH PLANNER

SUNDAY	MONDAY	TUESDAY	WEDNESDAY	THURSDAY	FRIDAY	SATURDAY
31 Halloween	1 All Saints' Day	2 All Souls' Day Day of the Dead	3	4 ●	5	6
7	8	9	10	11	12	13
14	15	16	17	18 Remembrance Day Veterans' Day ☆	19	20 ○
21	22	23	24	25	26	27
28 Hanukkah	29	30	1	2 Thanksgiving Day ☆	3	4 ●

DECEMBER – 2021 MONTH PLANNER

SUNDAY	MONDAY	TUESDAY	WEDNESDAY	THURSDAY	FRIDAY	SATURDAY
28	29	30	1	2	3	4
5	6 Hanukkah	7	8	9	10	11
12	13	14	15	16	17	18
19	20	21	22	23	24	25
26	27	28	29	30	31	1 New Year's Day
Boxing Day Kwanzaa ☆					New Year's Eve	Christmas Day

NOTES

THE YEAR

2021

MONDAY
28

TUESDAY
29

WEDNESDAY
30 ○

THURSDAY
31
NEW YEAR'S EVE

FRIDAY

1

NEW YEAR'S DAY

SATURDAY

2

SUNDAY

3

NOTES

DECEMBER

S	M	T	W	T	F	S
29	30	1	2	3	4	5
6	7	8	9	10	11	12
13	14	15	16	17	18	19
20	21	22	23	24	25	26
27	28	29	30	31	1	2

MONDAY
4

TUESDAY
5

WEDNESDAY
6 ☾

THURSDAY
7

FRIDAY
8

SATURDAY
9

SUNDAY
10

NOTES

JANUARY

S	M	T	W	T	F	S
27	28	29	30	31	1	2
3	4	5	6	7	8	9
10	11	12	13	14	15	16
17	18	19	20	21	22	23
24/31	25	26	27	28	29	30

JANUARY

MONDAY
11

TUESDAY
12

WEDNESDAY
13 ●

THURSDAY
14

FRIDAY
15

SATURDAY
16

SUNDAY
17

NOTES

JANUARY

S	M	T	W	T	F	S
27	28	29	30	31	1	2
3	4	5	6	7	8	9
10	11	12	13	14	15	16
17	18	19	20	21	22	23
24/31	25	26	27	28	29	30

MONDAY
18
MARTIN LUTHER KING JR.
DAY ☆

TUESDAY
19

WEDNESDAY
20 ☽

THURSDAY
21

2021

FRIDAY
22

SATURDAY
23

SUNDAY
24

NOTES

JANUARY

S	M	T	W	T	F	S
27	28	29	30	31	1	2
3	4	5	6	7	8	9
10	11	12	13	14	15	16
17	18	19	20	21	22	23
24/31	25	26	27	28	29	30

MONDAY
25

TUESDAY
26

WEDNESDAY
27

THURSDAY
28 ○

FRIDAY
29

SATURDAY
30

SUNDAY
31

NOTES

JANUARY

S	M	T	W	T	F	S
27	28	29	30	31	1	2
3	4	5	6	7	8	9
10	11	12	13	14	15	16
17	18	19	20	21	22	23
24/31	25	26	27	28	29	30

MONDAY
1

_____

TUESDAY
2
GROUNDHOG DAY

_____

WEDNESDAY
3

_____

THURSDAY
4 ☾

FRIDAY
5

SATURDAY
6

SUNDAY
7

NOTES

FEBRUARY

S	M	T	W	T	F	S
31	1	2	3	4	5	6
7	8	9	10	11	12	13
14	15	16	17	18	19	20
21	22	23	24	25	26	27
28	1	2	3	4	5	6

MONDAY
8

TUESDAY
9

WEDNESDAY
10

THURSDAY
11 ●

FRIDAY
12
CHINESE NEW YEAR

_____
_____
_____
_____
_____
_____
_____
_____

SATURDAY
13

_____
_____
_____
_____
_____
_____
_____
_____

SUNDAY
14
VALENTINE'S DAY

_____
_____
_____
_____
_____
_____
_____

NOTES

FEBRUARY

S	M	T	W	T	F	S
31	1	2	3	4	5	6
7	8	9	10	11	12	13
14	15	16	17	18	19	20
21	22	23	24	25	26	27
28	1	2	3	4	5	6

FEBRUARY

MONDAY
15
CIVIC HOLIDAY (AB BC MB
   NB NS ON PE SK) 🍁
PRESIDENTS' DAY ☆

TUESDAY
16
MARDI GRAS
SHROVE TUESDAY

WEDNESDAY
17
ASH WEDNESDAY

THURSDAY
18

2021

FRIDAY
19 ☽
HERITAGE DAY (YT) 🍁

SATURDAY
20

SUNDAY
21

NOTES

FEBRUARY

S	M	T	W	T	F	S
31	1	2	3	4	5	6
7	8	9	10	11	12	13
14	15	16	17	18	19	20
21	22	23	24	25	26	27
28	1	2	3	4	5	6

FEBRUARY

MONDAY
22

TUESDAY
23

WEDNESDAY
24

THURSDAY
25

FRIDAY
26
PURIM

SATURDAY
27 ○

SUNDAY
28

NOTES

			FEBRUARY			
S	M	T	W	T	F	S
31	1	2	3	4	5	6
7	8	9	10	11	12	13
14	15	16	17	18	19	20
21	22	23	24	25	26	27
28	1	2	3	4	5	6

MARCH

MONDAY
1

TUESDAY
2

WEDNESDAY
3

THURSDAY
4

FRIDAY
5

SATURDAY
6 ☾

SUNDAY
7

NOTES

MARCH

S	M	T	W	T	F	S
28	1	2	3	4	5	6
7	8	9	10	11	12	13
14	15	16	17	18	19	20
21	22	23	24	25	26	27
28	29	30	31	1	2	3

MONDAY
8

TUESDAY
9

WEDNESDAY
10

THURSDAY
11

FRIDAY
12

SATURDAY
13 ●

SUNDAY
14 ☺

NOTES

MARCH

S	M	T	W	T	F	S
28	1	2	3	4	5	6
7	8	9	10	11	12	13
14	15	16	17	18	19	20
21	22	23	24	25	26	27
28	29	30	31	1	2	3

MONDAY
15

TUESDAY
16

WEDNESDAY
17
ST. PATRICK'S DAY

THURSDAY
18

FRIDAY
19

SATURDAY
20 ✿
09:37 UTC

SUNDAY
21 ☽

NOTES

MARCH

S	M	T	W	T	F	S
28	1	2	3	4	5	6
7	8	9	10	11	12	13
14	15	16	17	18	19	20
21	22	23	24	25	26	27
28	29	30	31	1	2	3

MONDAY
22

TUESDAY
23

WEDNESDAY
24

THURSDAY
25

2021

FRIDAY
26

SATURDAY
27

SUNDAY
28 ○
PALM SUNDAY
PASSOVER

NOTES

MARCH

S	M	T	W	T	F	S
28	1	2	3	4	5	6
7	8	9	10	11	12	13
14	15	16	17	18	19	20
21	22	23	24	25	26	27
28	29	30	31	1	2	3

MONDAY
29

TUESDAY
30

WEDNESDAY
31

THURSDAY
1
APRIL FOOLS' DAY

FRIDAY
2
GOOD FRIDAY

SATURDAY
3

SUNDAY
4 ☾
EASTER

NOTES

APRIL

S	M	T	W	T	F	S
28	29	30	31	1	2	3
4	5	6	7	8	9	10
11	12	13	14	15	16	17
18	19	20	21	22	23	24
25	26	27	28	29	30	1

MONDAY
5
EASTER MONDAY 🍁

TUESDAY
6

WEDNESDAY
7

THURSDAY
8

FRIDAY
9

SATURDAY
10

SUNDAY
11

NOTES

APRIL

S	M	T	W	T	F	S
28	29	30	31	1	2	3
4	5	6	7	8	9	10
11	12	13	14	15	16	17
18	19	20	21	22	23	24
25	26	27	28	29	30	1

MONDAY
12 ●

TUESDAY
13
RAMADAN BEGINS

WEDNESDAY
14

THURSDAY
15

FRIDAY
16

SATURDAY
17

SUNDAY
18

NOTES

APRIL

S	M	T	W	T	F	S
28	29	30	31	1	2	3
4	5	6	7	8	9	10
11	12	13	14	15	16	17
18	19	20	21	22	23	24
25	26	27	28	29	30	1

MONDAY
19

TUESDAY
20 ☽

WEDNESDAY
21

THURSDAY
22
EARTH DAY

FRIDAY
23

SATURDAY
24

SUNDAY
25

NOTES

APRIL

S	M	T	W	T	F	S
28	29	30	31	1	2	3
4	5	6	7	8	9	10
11	12	13	14	15	16	17
18	19	20	21	22	23	24
25	26	27	28	29	30	1

MONDAY
26

TUESDAY
27 ○

WEDNESDAY
28

THURSDAY
29

FRIDAY
30

SATURDAY
1

SUNDAY
2

NOTES

APRIL

S	M	T	W	T	F	S
28	29	30	31	1	2	3
4	5	6	7	8	9	10
11	12	13	14	15	16	17
18	19	20	21	22	23	24
25	26	27	28	29	30	1

MONDAY
3 ☾

TUESDAY
4

WEDNESDAY
5
CINCO DE MAYO

THURSDAY
6

FRIDAY

7

SATURDAY

8

SUNDAY

9

MOTHER'S DAY

NOTES

MAY

S	M	T	W	T	F	S
25	26	27	28	29	30	1
2	3	4	5	6	7	8
9	10	11	12	13	14	15
16	17	18	19	20	21	22
23/30	24/31	25	26	27	28	29

MAY

MONDAY
10

TUESDAY
11 ●

WEDNESDAY
12

THURSDAY
13
EID AL-FITR

FRIDAY
14

SATURDAY
15

SUNDAY
16

NOTES

MAY

S	M	T	W	T	F	S
25	26	27	28	29	30	1
2	3	4	5	6	7	8
9	10	11	12	13	14	15
16	17	18	19	20	21	22
23/30	24/31	25	26	27	28	29

MONDAY
17
SHAVUOT

TUESDAY
18

WEDNESDAY
19 ☽

THURSDAY
20

FRIDAY
21

SATURDAY
22

SUNDAY
23

NOTES

MAY

S	M	T	W	T	F	S
25	26	27	28	29	30	1
2	3	4	5	6	7	8
9	10	11	12	13	14	15
16	17	18	19	20	21	22
23/30 24/31	25	26	27	28	29	

MAY

MONDAY
24

TUESDAY
25

WEDNESDAY
26 ○

THURSDAY
27

FRIDAY
28

_____

SATURDAY
29

_____

SUNDAY
30

_____

NOTES

MAY

S	M	T	W	T	F	S
25	26	27	28	29	30	1
2	3	4	5	6	7	8
9	10	11	12	13	14	15
16	17	18	19	20	21	22
23/30 24/31	25	26	27	28	29	

MAY–JUNE

MONDAY
31
MEMORIAL DAY ☆

TUESDAY
1

WEDNESDAY
2 ☾

THURSDAY
3

FRIDAY
4

SATURDAY
5

SUNDAY
6

NOTES

JUNE

S	M	T	W	T	F	S
30	31	1	2	3	4	5
6	7	8	9	10	11	12
13	14	15	16	17	18	19
20	21	22	23	24	25	26
27	28	29	30	1	2	3

JUNE

MONDAY
7

TUESDAY
8

WEDNESDAY
9

THURSDAY
10

FRIDAY

11

SATURDAY

12

SUNDAY

13

NOTES

JUNE

S	M	T	W	T	F	S
30	31	1	2	3	4	5
6	7	8	9	10	11	12
13	14	15	16	17	18	19
20	21	22	23	24	25	26
27	28	29	30	1	2	3

MONDAY
14
FLAG DAY ☆

TUESDAY
15

WEDNESDAY
16

THURSDAY
17

FRIDAY
18 ☽

SATURDAY
19
JUNETEENTH ☆

SUNDAY
20
FATHER'S DAY

NOTES

JUNE

S	M	T	W	T	F	S
30	31	1	2	3	4	5
6	7	8	9	10	11	12
13	14	15	16	17	18	19
20	21	22	23	24	25	26
27	28	29	30	1	2	3

MONDAY
21 ☼

03:32 UTC
NATIONAL ABORIGINAL
DAY (NT YT) 🍁
DISCOVERY DAY (NL) 🍁

TUESDAY
22

WEDNESDAY
23

THURSDAY
24 ○

ST. JEAN BAPTISTE DAY
(QC) 🍁

FRIDAY
25

SATURDAY
26

SUNDAY
27

NOTES

			JUNE			
S	M	T	W	T	F	S
30	31	1	2	3	4	5
6	7	8	9	10	11	12
13	14	15	16	17	18	19
20	21	22	23	24	25	26
27	28	29	30	1	2	3

MONDAY
28

TUESDAY
29

WEDNESDAY
30

THURSDAY
1 ☾
CANADA DAY 🍁

FRIDAY
2

SATURDAY
3

SUNDAY
4
INDEPENDENCE DAY ☆

NOTES

JULY

S	M	T	W	T	F	S
27	28	29	30	1	2	3
4	5	6	7	8	9	10
11	12	13	14	15	16	17
18	19	20	21	22	23	24
25	26	27	28	29	30	31

JULY

MONDAY
5

TUESDAY
6

WEDNESDAY
7

THURSDAY
8

FRIDAY
9
NUNAVUT DAY (NU) 🍁

SATURDAY
10 ●

SUNDAY
11

NOTES

JULY

S	M	T	W	T	F	S
27	28	29	30	1	2	3
4	5	6	7	8	9	10
11	12	13	14	15	16	17
18	19	20	21	22	23	24
25	26	27	28	29	30	31

MONDAY
12

TUESDAY
13

WEDNESDAY
14

THURSDAY
15

FRIDAY
16

SATURDAY
17 ☽

SUNDAY
18

NOTES

JULY						
S	M	T	W	T	F	S
27	28	29	30	1	2	3
4	5	6	7	8	9	10
11	12	13	14	15	16	17
18	19	20	21	22	23	24
25	26	27	28	29	30	31

JULY

MONDAY
19

TUESDAY
20
EID AL-ADHA

WEDNESDAY
21

THURSDAY
22

2021

FRIDAY
23

SATURDAY
24 ○

SUNDAY
25

NOTES

JULY

S	M	T	W	T	F	S
27	28	29	30	1	2	3
4	5	6	7	8	9	10
11	12	13	14	15	16	17
18	19	20	21	22	23	24
25	26	27	28	29	30	31

MONDAY
26

TUESDAY
27

WEDNESDAY
28

THURSDAY
29

2021

FRIDAY
30

SATURDAY
31 ☾

SUNDAY
1

NOTES

JULY

S	M	T	W	T	F	S
27	28	29	30	1	2	3
4	5	6	7	8	9	10
11	12	13	14	15	16	17
18	19	20	21	22	23	24
25	26	27	28	29	30	31

AUGUST

MONDAY
2
CIVIC HOLIDAY 🍁

TUESDAY
3

WEDNESDAY
4

THURSDAY
5

FRIDAY
6

SATURDAY
7

SUNDAY
8 ●

NOTES

AUGUST

S	M	T	W	T	F	S
1	2	3	4	5	6	7
8	9	10	11	12	13	14
15	16	17	18	19	20	21
22	23	24	25	26	27	28
29	30	31	1	2	3	4

MONDAY
9
MUHARRAM BEGINS

TUESDAY
10

WEDNESDAY
11

THURSDAY
12

FRIDAY
13

SATURDAY
14

SUNDAY
15 ☽

NOTES

AUGUST

S	M	T	W	T	F	S
1	2	3	4	5	6	7
8	9	10	11	12	13	14
15	16	17	18	19	20	21
22	23	24	25	26	27	28
29	30	31	1	2	3	4

MONDAY
16
DISCOVERY DAY (YT) 🍁

TUESDAY
17

WEDNESDAY
18

THURSDAY
19

FRIDAY
20

SATURDAY
21

SUNDAY
22 ○

NOTES

AUGUST

S	M	T	W	T	F	S
1	2	3	4	5	6	7
8	9	10	11	12	13	14
15	16	17	18	19	20	21
22	23	24	25	26	27	28
29	30	31	1	2	3	4

AUGUST

MONDAY
23

TUESDAY
24

WEDNESDAY
25

THURSDAY
26

FRIDAY
27

SATURDAY
28

SUNDAY
29

NOTES

AUGUST

S	M	T	W	T	F	S
1	2	3	4	5	6	7
8	9	10	11	12	13	14
15	16	17	18	19	20	21
22	23	24	25	26	27	28
29	30	31	1	2	3	4

MONDAY
30 ☾

TUESDAY
31

WEDNESDAY
1

THURSDAY
2

2021

FRIDAY
3

SATURDAY
4

SUNDAY
5

NOTES

SEPTEMBER

S	M	T	W	T	F	S
29	30	31	1	2	3	4
5	6	7	8	9	10	11
12	13	14	15	16	17	18
19	20	21	22	23	24	25
26	27	28	29	30	1	2

MONDAY
6
LABOUR DAY

TUESDAY
7 ●
ROSH HASHANAH

WEDNESDAY
8

THURSDAY
9

2021

FRIDAY
10

SATURDAY
11

SUNDAY
12

NOTES

SEPTEMBER

S	M	T	W	T	F	S
29	30	31	1	2	3	4
5	6	7	8	9	10	11
12	13	14	15	16	17	18
19	20	21	22	23	24	25
26	27	28	29	30	1	2

MONDAY
13 ☽

TUESDAY
14

WEDNESDAY
15

THURSDAY
16
YOM KIPPUR

FRIDAY
17

SATURDAY
18

SUNDAY
19

NOTES

SEPTEMBER

S	M	T	W	T	F	S
29	30	31	1	2	3	4
5	6	7	8	9	10	11
12	13	14	15	16	17	18
19	20	21	22	23	24	25
26	27	28	29	30	1	2

SEPTEMBER

MONDAY
20 ○

TUESDAY
21
SUKKOT

WEDNESDAY
22
19:21 UTC

THURSDAY
23

2021

FRIDAY
24

SATURDAY
25

SUNDAY
26

NOTES

SEPTEMBER

S	M	T	W	T	F	S
29	30	31	1	2	3	4
5	6	7	8	9	10	11
12	13	14	15	16	17	18
19	20	21	22	23	24	25
26	27	28	29	30	1	2

MONDAY
27

TUESDAY
28

WEDNESDAY
29 ☾

THURSDAY
30

2021

FRIDAY

1

SATURDAY

2

SUNDAY

3

NOTES

SEPTEMBER

S	M	T	W	T	F	S
29	30	31	1	2	3	4
5	6	7	8	9	10	11
12	13	14	15	16	17	18
19	20	21	22	23	24	25
26	27	28	29	30	1	2

MONDAY
4

TUESDAY
5

WEDNESDAY
6 ●

THURSDAY
7

FRIDAY
8

SATURDAY
9

SUNDAY
10

NOTES

S	M	T	W	T	F	S
26	27	28	29	30	1	2
3	4	5	6	7	8	9
10	11	12	13	14	15	16
17	18	19	20	21	22	23
24/31	25	26	27	28	29	30

OCTOBER

MONDAY
11
THANKSGIVING DAY 🍁
COLUMBUS DAY ☆

TUESDAY
12

WEDNESDAY
13 ☽

THURSDAY
14

FRIDAY
15

SATURDAY
16

SUNDAY
17

NOTES

OCTOBER

S	M	T	W	T	F	S
26	27	28	29	30	1	2
3	4	5	6	7	8	9
10	11	12	13	14	15	16
17	18	19	20	21	22	23
24/31	25	26	27	28	29	30

MONDAY
18
MAWLID AL-NABI

TUESDAY
19

WEDNESDAY
20 ○

THURSDAY
21

FRIDAY
22

_____

SATURDAY
23

_____

SUNDAY
24

_____

NOTES

OCTOBER

S	M	T	W	T	F	S
26	27	28	29	30	1	2
3	4	5	6	7	8	9
10	11	12	13	14	15	16
17	18	19	20	21	22	23
24/31	25	26	27	28	29	30

MONDAY
25

TUESDAY
26

WEDNESDAY
27

THURSDAY
28 ☾

FRIDAY
29

SATURDAY
30

SUNDAY
31
HALLOWEEN

NOTES

OCTOBER

S	M	T	W	T	F	S
26	27	28	29	30	1	2
3	4	5	6	7	8	9
10	11	12	13	14	15	16
17	18	19	20	21	22	23
24/31	25	26	27	28	29	30

MONDAY
1
ALL SAINTS' DAY

TUESDAY
2
ALL SOULS' DAY
DAY OF THE DEAD

WEDNESDAY
3

THURSDAY
4

2021

FRIDAY
5

SATURDAY
6

SUNDAY
7 ⊘

NOTES

NOVEMBER

MONDAY
8

TUESDAY
9

WEDNESDAY
10

THURSDAY
11 ☽
REMEMBRANCE DAY 🍁
VETERANS' DAY ☆

2021

FRIDAY
12

SATURDAY
13

SUNDAY
14

NOTES

NOVEMBER

S	M	T	W	T	F	S
31	1	2	3	4	5	6
7	8	9	10	11	12	13
14	15	16	17	18	19	20
21	22	23	24	25	26	27
28	29	30	1	2	3	4

MONDAY
15

TUESDAY
16

WEDNESDAY
17

THURSDAY
18

2021

FRIDAY
19 ○

_____
_____
_____
_____
_____
_____

SATURDAY
20

_____
_____
_____
_____
_____
_____

SUNDAY
21

_____
_____
_____
_____
_____

NOTES

NOVEMBER

S	M	T	W	T	F	S
31	1	2	3	4	5	6
7	8	9	10	11	12	13
14	15	16	17	18	19	20
21	22	23	24	25	26	27
28	29	30	1	2	3	4

NOVEMBER

MONDAY
22

TUESDAY
23

WEDNESDAY
24

THURSDAY
25
THANKSGIVING DAY ☆

2021

FRIDAY
26

SATURDAY
27 ☾

SUNDAY
28

NOTES

NOVEMBER

S	M	T	W	T	F	S
31	1	2	3	4	5	6
7	8	9	10	11	12	13
14	15	16	17	18	19	20
21	22	23	24	25	26	27
28	29	30	1	2	3	4

MONDAY
29
HANUKKAH

TUESDAY
30

WEDNESDAY
1

THURSDAY
2

FRIDAY
3

SATURDAY
4 ●

SUNDAY
5

NOTES

DECEMBER

S	M	T	W	T	F	S
28	29	30	1	2	3	4
5	6	7	8	9	10	11
12	13	14	15	16	17	18
19	20	21	22	23	24	25
26	27	28	29	30	31	1

DECEMBER

MONDAY
6

TUESDAY
7

WEDNESDAY
8

THURSDAY
9

FRIDAY
10

SATURDAY
11 ☽

SUNDAY
12

NOTES

DECEMBER

S	M	T	W	T	F	S
28	29	30	1	2	3	4
5	6	7	8	9	10	11
12	13	14	15	16	17	18
19	20	21	22	23	24	25
26	27	28	29	30	31	1

DECEMBER

MONDAY
13

TUESDAY
14

WEDNESDAY
15

THURSDAY
16

FRIDAY
17

SATURDAY
18

SUNDAY
19 ○

NOTES

DECEMBER

S	M	T	W	T	F	S
28	29	30	1	2	3	4
5	6	7	8	9	10	11
12	13	14	15	16	17	18
19	20	21	22	23	24	25
26	27	28	29	30	31	1

MONDAY
20

TUESDAY
21 ☀
15:59 UTC

WEDNESDAY
22

THURSDAY
23

FRIDAY
24

SATURDAY
25
CHRISTMAS DAY

SUNDAY
26
BOXING DAY 🍁
KWANZAA ☆

NOTES

DECEMBER

S	M	T	W	T	F	S
28	29	30	1	2	3	4
5	6	7	8	9	10	11
12	13	14	15	16	17	18
19	20	21	22	23	24	25
26	27	28	29	30	31	1

MONDAY
27 ☾

TUESDAY
28

WEDNESDAY
29

THURSDAY
30

FRIDAY
31
NEW YEAR'S EVE

SATURDAY
1
NEW YEAR'S DAY

SUNDAY
2 ●

NOTES

DECEMBER

S	M	T	W	T	F	S
28	29	30	1	2	3	4
5	6	7	8	9	10	11
12	13	14	15	16	17	18
19	20	21	22	23	24	25
26	27	28	29	30	31	1

INTERNATIONAL HOLIDAYS 2021

AUSTRALIA

January 1	New Year's Day
26	Australia Day
April 2	Good Friday
3	Easter Saturday*
4	Easter
5	Easter Monday
25	Anzac Day
June 14	Queen's Birthday*
December 25	Christmas Day
26	Boxing Day

AUSTRIA

January 1	New Year's Day
6	Epiphany
April 2	Good Friday*
4	Easter
5	Easter Monday
May 1	Labour Day
13	Ascension
24	Whit Monday
June 3	Corpus Christi Day
August 15	Assumption
October 26	National Day
November 1	All Saints' Day
December 8	Immaculate Conception
25	Christmas Day
26	St. Stephen's Day

BELGIUM

January 1	New Year's Day
April 4	Easter
5	Easter Monday
May 1	Labour Day
13	Ascension
24	Whit Monday
July 21	National Day
August 15	Assumption
November 1	All Saints' Day
11	Armistice Day
December 25	Christmas Day

CZECH REPUBLIC

January 1	New Year's Day
April 2	Good Friday
4	Easter
5	Easter Monday
May 1	May Day
8	Liberation Day
July 5	St. Cyril and St. Methodius Day
6	Jan Hus Day
September 28	Statehood Day
October 28	Independence Day
November 17	Freedom and Democracy Day
December 24	Christmas Eve
25	Christmas Day
26	Second Christmas Day

FRANCE

January 1	New Year's Day
April 4	Easter
5	Easter Monday
May 1	Labour Day
8	WWII Victory Day
13	Ascension
24	Whit Monday
July 14	National Day
August 15	Assumption
November 1	All Saints' Day
11	Armistice Day
December 25	Christmas Day

GERMANY

January 1	New Year's Day
April 2	Good Friday
4	Easter
5	Easter Monday
May 1	Labour Day
13	Ascension
24	Whit Monday
October 3	Day of German Unity
December 25	Christmas Day
26	Second Christmas Day

IRELAND

January 1	New Year's Day
March 17	St. Patrick's Day
April 2	Good Friday
4	Easter
5	Easter Monday
May 3	May Bank Holiday
June 7	June Bank Holiday

INTERNATIONAL HOLIDAYS 2021

August 2 August Bank Holiday
October 25 October Bank Holiday
December 25 Christmas Day
26 St. Stephen's Day

ITALY

January 1 New Year's Day
6 Epiphany
April 4 Easter
5 Easter Monday
25 Liberation Day
May 1 Labour Day
June 2 Republic Day
August 15 Assumption
November 1 All Saints' Day
December 8 Immaculate Conception
25 Christmas Day
26 St. Stephen's Day

JAPAN

January 1 New Year's Day
11 Coming of Age Day
February 11 National Foundation Day
23 Emperor's Birthday
March 20 Spring Equinox
April 29 Showa Day
May 3 Constitution Memorial Day
4 Greenery Day
5 Children's Day
July 19 Marine Day
August 11 Mountain Day
September 20 Respect for the Aged Day
23 Autumn Equinox
October 11 Sports Day
November 3 Culture Day
23 Labour Thanksgiving Day

NETHERLANDS

January 1 New Year's Day
April 2 Good Friday*
4 Easter
5 Easter Monday
27 King's Birthday
May 5 Liberation Day
13 Ascension
23 Pentecost
24 Whit Monday

December 25 Christmas Day
26 Second Christmas Day

NORWAY

January 1 New Year's Day
April 1 Maundy Thursday
2 Good Friday
4 Easter
5 Easter Monday
May 1 Labour Day
13 Ascension
17 Constitution Day
23 Whit Sunday
24 Whit Monday
December 25 Christmas Day
26 Second Christmas Day

POLAND

January 1 New Year's Day
6 Epiphany
April 4 Easter
5 Easter Monday
May 1 State Holiday
3 Constitution Day
23 Pentecost
June 3 Corpus Christi Day
August 15 Assumption
November 1 All Saints' Day
11 Independence Day
December 25 Christmas Day
26 Second Christmas Day

PORTUGAL

January 1 New Year's Day
February 16 Shrove Tuesday (Carnival)
April 2 Good Friday
4 Easter
25 Liberation Day
May 1 Labour Day
June 3 Corpus Christi Day
10 National Day
August 15 Assumption
October 5 Republic Day
November 1 All Saints' Day
December 1 Independence Day
8 Immaculate Conception
25 Christmas Day

INTERNATIONAL HOLIDAYS 2021

SLOVAKIA

January 1	New Year's Day
	Republic Day
6	Epiphany
April 2	Good Friday
4	Easter
5	Easter Monday
May 1	May Day
8	Victory Day
July 5	St. Cyril and St. Methodius Day
August 29	Slovak National Uprising Day
September 1	Constitution Day
15	Our Lady of Sorrows Day
November 1	All Saints' Day
17	Freedom and Democracy Day
December 24	Christmas Eve
25	Christmas Day
26	Second Christmas Day

SPAIN

January 1	New Year's Day
6	Epiphany
April 1	Maundy Thursday*
2	Good Friday
May 1	Labour Day
August 15	Assumption
October 12	National Day
November 1	All Saints' Day
December 6	Constitution Day
8	Immaculate Conception
25	Christmas Day

SWEDEN

January 1	New Year's Day
6	Epiphany
April 2	Good Friday
4	Easter
5	Easter Monday
May 1	Labour Day
13	Ascension
23	Pentecost
June 6	National Day
26	Midsummer's Day
November 6	All Saints' Day
December 25	Christmas Day
26	Second Christmas Day

SWITZERLAND

January 1	New Year's Day
April 2	Good Friday*
4	Easter
5	Easter Monday*
May 1	Labour Day*
13	Ascension
24	Whit Monday*
August 1	National Day
December 25	Christmas Day
26	St. Stephen's Day*

UNITED KINGDOM

January 1	New Year's Day
2	Second of January*
March 17	St. Patrick's Day*
April 2	Good Friday
4	Easter
5	Easter Monday*
May 3	Early May Bank Holiday
31	Spring Bank Holiday
August 2	Summer Bank Holiday*
30	Summer Bank Holiday*
November 30	St. Andrew's Day*
December 25	Christmas Day
26	Boxing Day

Not a public holiday/Not a public holiday in all regions.
This table lists commemorative dates. Additional public holidays may precede or follow some dates.
Regional holidays may not be included. This information is provided as a guide only.

NOTES

NOTES

2022

JANUARY

S	M	T	W	T	F	S
26	27	28	29	30	31	1
2	3	4	5	6	7	8
9	10	11	12	13	14	15
16	17	18	19	20	21	22
23/30	24/31	25	26	27	28	29

FEBRUARY

S	M	T	W	T	F	S
30	31	1	2	3	4	5
6	7	8	9	10	11	12
13	14	15	16	17	18	19
20	21	22	23	24	25	26
27	28	1	2	3	4	5

MARCH

S	M	T	W	T	F	S
27	28	1	2	3	4	5
6	7	8	9	10	11	12
13	14	15	16	17	18	19
20	21	22	23	24	25	26
27	28	29	30	31	1	2

APRIL

S	M	T	W	T	F	S
27	28	29	30	31	1	2
3	4	5	6	7	8	9
10	11	12	13	14	15	16
17	18	19	20	21	22	23
24	25	26	27	28	29	30

MAY

S	M	T	W	T	F	S
1	2	3	4	5	6	7
8	9	10	11	12	13	14
15	16	17	18	19	20	21
22	23	24	25	26	27	28
29	30	31	1	2	3	4

JUNE

S	M	T	W	T	F	S
29	30	31	1	2	3	4
5	6	7	8	9	10	11
12	13	14	15	16	17	18
19	20	21	22	23	24	25
26	27	28	29	30	1	2

JULY

S	M	T	W	T	F	S
26	27	28	29	30	1	2
3	4	5	6	7	8	9
10	11	12	13	14	15	16
17	18	19	20	21	22	23
24/31	25	26	27	28	29	30

AUGUST

S	M	T	W	T	F	S
31	1	2	3	4	5	6
7	8	9	10	11	12	13
14	15	16	17	18	19	20
21	22	23	24	25	26	27
28	29	30	31	1	2	3

SEPTEMBER

S	M	T	W	T	F	S
28	29	30	31	1	2	3
4	5	6	7	8	9	10
11	12	13	14	15	16	17
18	19	20	21	22	23	24
25	26	27	28	29	30	1

OCTOBER

S	M	T	W	T	F	S
25	26	27	28	29	30	1
2	3	4	5	6	7	8
9	10	11	12	13	14	15
16	17	18	19	20	21	22
23/30	24/31	25	26	27	28	29

NOVEMBER

S	M	T	W	T	F	S
30	31	1	2	3	4	5
6	7	8	9	10	11	12
13	14	15	16	17	18	19
20	21	22	23	24	25	26
27	28	29	30	1	2	3

DECEMBER

S	M	T	W	T	F	S
27	28	29	30	1	2	3
4	5	6	7	8	9	10
11	12	13	14	15	16	17
18	19	20	21	22	23	24
25	26	27	28	29	30	31

NATIONAL HOLIDAYS & CELEBRATIONS 2022

JANUARY

Saturday 1 New Year's Day
Monday 17 Martin Luther King Jr. Day ☆

FEBRUARY

Tuesday 1 Chinese New Year
Wednesday 2 Groundhog Day
Monday 14 Valentine's Day
Monday 21 Civic Holiday ♣
Presidents' Day ☆

MARCH

Tuesday 1 Mardi Gras
Shrove Tuesday
Wednesday 2 Ash Wednesday
Thursday 17 St. Patrick's Day
Purim*

APRIL

Friday 1 April Fools' Day
Saturday 2 Ramadan begins
Sunday 10 Palm Sunday
Friday 15 Good Friday
Saturday 16 Passover*
Sunday 17 Easter
Monday 18 Easter Monday ♣
Friday 22 Earth Day

MAY

Monday 2 Eid al-Fitr*
Thursday 5 Cinco de Mayo
Sunday 8 Mother's Day
Monday 23 Victoria Day ♣
Monday 30 Memorial Day ☆

JUNE

Sunday 5 Shavuot
Tuesday 14 Flag Day ☆

Sunday 19 Father's Day
Juneteenth ☆

JULY

Friday 1 Canada Day ♣
Monday 4 Independence Day ☆
Saturday 9 Eid al-Adha*
Saturday 30 Muharram begins

AUGUST

Monday 1 Civic Holiday ♣

SEPTEMBER

Monday 5 Labour Day
Monday 26 Rosh Hashanah*

OCTOBER

Wednesday 5 Yom Kippur
Saturday 8 Mawlid al-Nabi
Monday 10 Thanksgiving Day ♣
Columbus Day ☆
Sukkot*
Monday 31 Halloween

NOVEMBER

Tuesday 1 All Saints' Day
Wednesday 2 All Souls' Day
Day of the Dead
Friday 11 Remembrance Day ♣
Veterans' Day ☆
Thursday 24 Thanksgiving Day ☆

DECEMBER

Monday 19 Hanukkah*
Sunday 25 Christmas Day
Monday 26 Boxing Day ♣
Kwanzaa* ☆
Saturday 31 New Year's Eve

♣Canadian holidays ☆American holidays and celebrations
*Additional public holidays may precede or follow this date.

NOTES

2022 YEAR PLANNER

	JANUARY		FEBRUARY		MARCH
1	S	New Year's Day	T	Chinese New Year	T	Mardi Gras Shrove Tuesday
2	S		W	Groundhog Day	W	Ash Wednesday
3	M		T		T	
4	T		F		F	
5	W		S		S	
6	T		S		S	
7	F		M		M	
8	S		T		T	
9	S		W		W	
10	M		T		T	
11	T		F		F	
12	W		S		S	
13	T		S		S	☺
14	F		M	Valentine's Day	M	
15	S		T		T	
16	S		W		W	
17	M	Martin Luther King Jr. Day ☆	T		T	St. Patrick's Day Purim
18	T		F	Heritage Day (YT) 🍁	F	
19	W		S		S	
20	T		S		S	❀
21	F		M	Civic Holiday 🍁 Presidents' Day ☆	M	
22	S		T		T	
23	S		W		W	
24	M		T		T	
25	T		F		F	
26	W		S		S	
27	T		S		S	
28	F		M		M	
29	S				T	
30	S				W	
31	M				T	

2022 YEAR PLANNER

	APRIL		MAY		JUNE
1	F	April Fools' Day	S		W
2	S	Ramadan begins	M	Eid al-Fitr	T
3	S		T		F
4	M		W		S
5	T		T	Cinco de Mayo	S — Shavuot
6	W		F		M
7	T		S		T
8	F		S	Mother's Day	W
9	S		M		T
10	S	Palm Sunday	T		F
11	M		W		S
12	T		T		S
13	W		F		M
14	T		S		T — Flag Day ☆
15	F	Good Friday	S		W
16	S	Passover	M		T
17	S	Easter	T		F
18	M	Easter Monday ◆	W		S
19	T		T		S — Father's Day / Juneteenth ☆
20	W		F		M
21	T		S		T — National Aboriginal Day (NT YT) ◆ ✿
22	F	Earth Day	S		W
23	S		M	Victoria Day ◆	T
24	S		T		F — St. Jean Baptiste Day (QC) ◆
25	M		W		S
26	T		T		S
27	W		F		M — Discovery Day (NL) ◆
28	T		S		T
29	F		S		W
30	S		M	Memorial Day ☆	T
31			T		

2022 YEAR PLANNER

		JULY			AUGUST			SEPTEMBER
1	F	Canada Day 🍁	M		Civic Holiday 🍁	T		
2	S		T			F		
3	S		W			S		
4	M	Independence Day ☆	T			S		
5	T		F			M		Labour Day
6	W		S			T		
7	T		S			W		
8	F		M			T		
9	S	Eid al-Adha Nunavut Day (NU) 🍁	T			F		
10	S		W			S		
11	M		T			S		
12	T		F			M		
13	W		S			T		
14	T		S			W		
15	F		M		Discovery Day (YT) 🍁	T		
16	S		T			F		
17	S		W			S		
18	M		T			S		
19	T		F			M		
20	W		S			T		
21	T		S			W		
22	F		M			T		
23	S		T			F		🍃
24	S		W			S		
25	M		T			S		
26	T		F			M		Rosh Hashanah
27	W		S			T		
28	T		S			W		
29	F		M			T		
30	S	Muharram begins	T			F		
31	S		W					

2O22 YEAR PLANNER

	OCTOBER		NOVEMBER		DECEMBER
1	S	T	All Saints' Day	T	
2	S	W	All Souls' Day / Day of the Dead	F	
3	M	T		S	
4	T	F		S	
5	W	Yom Kippur	S		M	
6	T	S	☺	T	
7	F	M		W	
8	S	Mawlid al-Nabi	T		T	
9	S	W		F	
10	M	Thanksgiving Day ♣ / Columbus Day ☆ /Sukkot	T		S	
11	T	F	Remembrance Day ♣ / Veterans' Day ☆	S	
12	W	S		M	
13	T	S		T	
14	F	M		W	
15	S	T		T	
16	S	W		F	
17	M	T		S	
18	T	F		S	
19	W	S		M	Hanukkah
20	T	S		T	
21	F	M		W	✳
22	S	T		T	
23	S	W		F	
24	M	T	Thanksgiving Day ☆	S	
25	T	F		S	Christmas Day
26	W	S		M	Boxing Day ♣ / Kwanzaa ☆
27	T	S		T	
28	F	M		W	
29	S	T		T	
30	S	W		F	
31	M	Halloween			S	New Year's Eve

INTERNATIONAL DIALING CODES

COUNTRY/AREA	DIAL OUT (ACCESS CODE)	DIAL IN (COUNTRY CODE)	EMERG. NUMBER	COUNTRY/AREA	DIAL OUT (ACCESS CODE)	DIAL IN (COUNTRY CODE)	EMERG. NUMBER
Algeria	00	213	17	Korea (South)	001*	82	999
Argentina	00	54	101	Latvia	00	371	112
Australia	0011	61	000	Lithuania	00	370	112
Austria	00	43	112	Luxembourg	00	352	112
Belgium	00	32	112	Macedonia	00	389	112
Bermuda	011	1441	911	Malaysia	00	60	999
Bolivia	00	591	110	Malta	00	356	112
Brazil	00	55	190	Mexico	00	52	066
Bulgaria	00	359	112	Morocco	00	212	19
Canada	011	1	911	Netherlands	00	31	112
Chile	00	56	133	New Zealand	00	64	111
China	00	86	110	Norway	00	47	112
Colombia	009*	57	112	Pakistan	00	92	15
Costa Rica	00	506	911	Paraguay	00	595	911
Croatia	00	385	112	Peru	00	51	105
Cuba	119	53	106	Philippines	00	63	117
Czech Republic	00	420	112	Poland	00	48	112
Denmark	00	45	112	Portugal	00	351	112
Dominican Repub.	011	1809	911	Puerto Rico	011	1787*	911
Ecuador	00	593	911	Qatar	00	974	999
Egypt	00	20	122	Romania	00	40	112
Estonia	00	372	112	Russia	810	7	112
Finland	00*	358	112	Saudi Arabia	00	966	999
France	00	33	112	Slovakia	00	421	112
Georgia	00	995	112	Slovenia	00	386	112
Germany	00	49	112	South Africa	00	27	10111
Greece	00	30	112	Spain	00	34	112
Guatemala	00	502	110	Sweden	00	46	112
Honduras	00	504	199	Switzerland	00	41	112
Hungary	00	36	112	Syria	00	963	112
Iceland	00	354	112	Thailand	001	66	191
India	00	91	100	Tunisia	00	216	197
Iran	00	98	110	Turkey	00	90	155
Ireland (Republic)	00	353	112	U.A.E.	00	971	999
Israel	00*	972	100	Ukraine	00	380	112
Italy	00	39	112	United Kingdom	00	44	112
Jamaica	011	1876	119	United States	011	1	911
Japan	010	81	110	Uruguay	00	598	911
Jordan	00	962	911	Venezuela	00	58	171

Additional access codes also in use.

WORLD TIME ZONES

UTC 12:00 PM	UTC+1 1:00 PM	UTC+2 2:00 PM	UTC+3 3:00 PM
Accra	Berlin	Athens	Baghdad
Lisbon	Paris	Cairo	Nairobi
London	Rome	Tel Aviv	Riyadh
UTC+4 4:00 PM	**UTC+5 5:00 PM**	**UTC+5.5 5:30 PM**	**UTC+6 6:00 PM**
Dubai	Karachi	Delhi	Almaty
Moscow	Tashkent	Kolkata	Dhaka
		Mumbai	
UTC+7 7:00 PM	**UTC+8 8:00 PM**	**UTC+9 9:00 PM**	**UTC+10 10:00 PM**
Bangkok	Beijing	Seoul	Melbourne
Jakarta	Manila	Tokyo	Sydney
	Singapore		
UTC+12 12:00 AM	**UTC−10 2:00 AM**	**UTC−9 3:00 AM**	**UTC−8 4:00 AM**
Auckland	Honolulu	Anchorage	Los Angeles
Suva			San Francisco
Wellington			Vancouver
UTC−6 6:00 AM	**UTC−5 7:00 AM**	**UTC−4 8:00 AM**	**UTC−3 9:00 AM**
Chicago	Miami	Halifax	Buenos Aires
Houston	New York	La Paz	Rio de Janeiro
Mexico City	Toronto	Santiago	

Coordinated Universal Time (UTC) is equivalent to Greenwich Mean Time (GMT).

CONVERSIONS

CLOTHING SIZES

WOMEN – CLOTHING						
France/Spain	34	36	38	40	42	44	46
Germany	32	34	36	38	40	42	44
Italy	36	38	40	42	44	46	48
Japan	5	7	9	11	13	15	17
North America	0	2	4	6	8	10	12
UK/Ireland	4	6	8	10	12	14	16

WOMEN – SHOES						
Europe	35	36	37	38	39	40	41
Japan	22	23	23.5	24	24.5	25.5	26
North America	5	6	6.5	7.5	8.5	9.5	10
UK/Ireland	2.5	3.5	4	5	6	7	7.5

MEN – SUITS AND COATS						
Europe	44	46	48	50	52	54	56
Japan	S	S	M	L	L	XL	XL
N. America/UK/Ire.	34	36	38	40	42	44	46

MEN – SHOES						
Europe	40	41	42	43	44	45	46
Japan	25.5	26	26.5	27.5	28	29	29.5
North America	7.5	8	8.5	9.5	10	11	11.5
UK/Ireland	7	7.5	8	9	9.5	10.5	11

These measurements may vary between different countries and manufacturers. They are provided as a guide only.

MEASUREMENTS

WEIGHT	
1 kilogram	2.2 pounds
1 pound	0.45 kilograms

VOLUME	
1 litre	0.26 gallons
1 gallon (US)	3.78 litres
1 gallon (US)	0.03 barrels

LENGTH/DISTANCE	
1 centimetre	0.39 inches
1 inch	2.54 centimetres
1 metre	39.37 inches
1 foot	30.48 centimetres
1 kilometre	0.62 miles
1 mile	1.6 kilometres
1 metre	1.09 yards
1 yard	91.44 cm

AREA	
1 sq metre	10.76 sq feet
1 sq foot	0.09 sq metres
1 sq metre	1.2 sq yards
1 sq yard	0.84 sq metres
1 hectare	2.47 acres
1 acre	0.4 hectares

TEMPERATURE

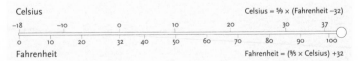

Celsius = $\frac{5}{9} \times$ (Fahrenheit −32)

Fahrenheit = ($\frac{9}{5} \times$ Celsius) +32

TRAVEL PLANNING

DATE FROM/TO	DESTINATION

BIRTHDAYS & IMPORTANT DATES

DATE	EVENT

☎   📱

✉

@

☎   📱

✉

@

☎   📱

✉

@

☎   📱

✉

@

☎   📱

✉

@

☎   📱

✉

@

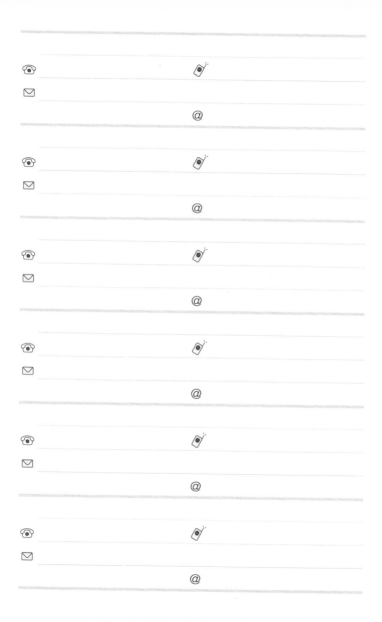

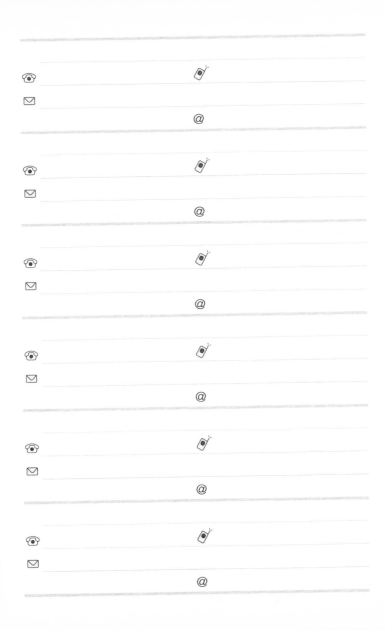

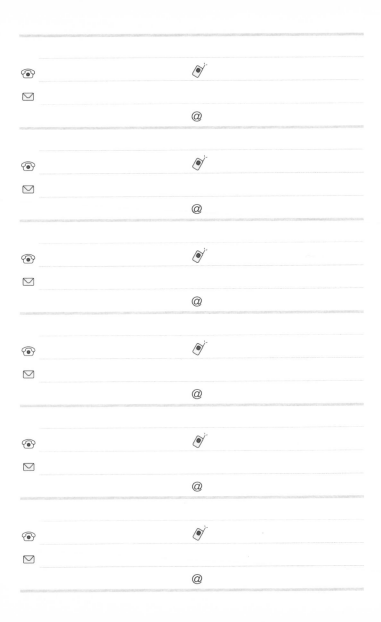

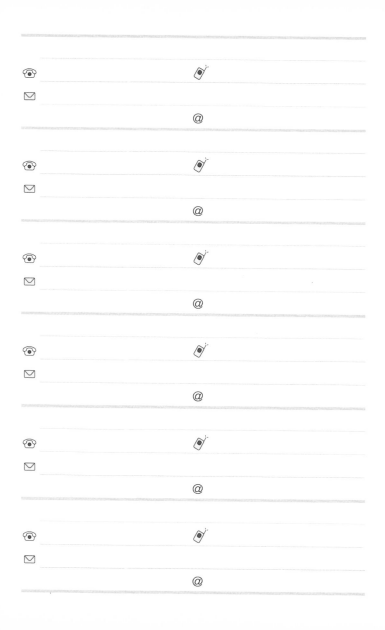

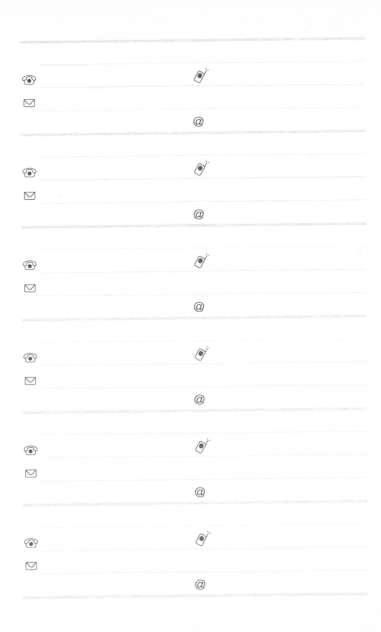

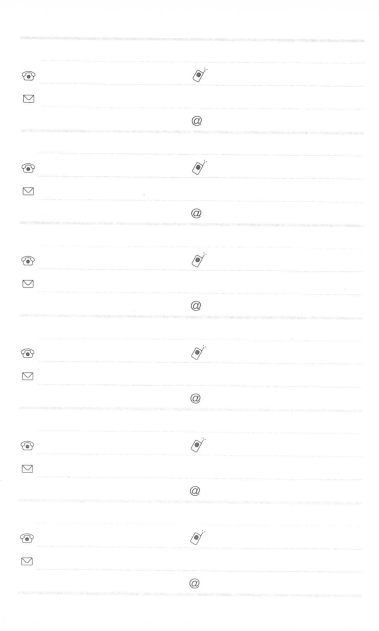

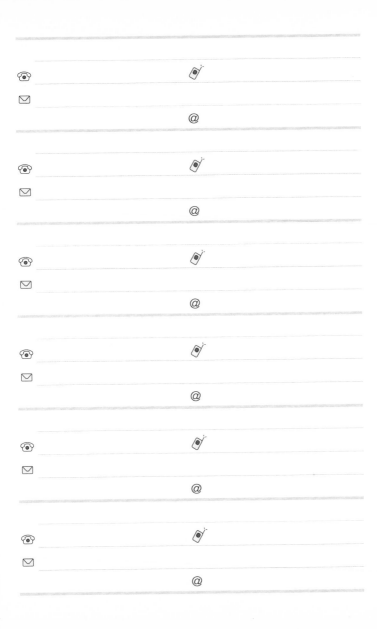

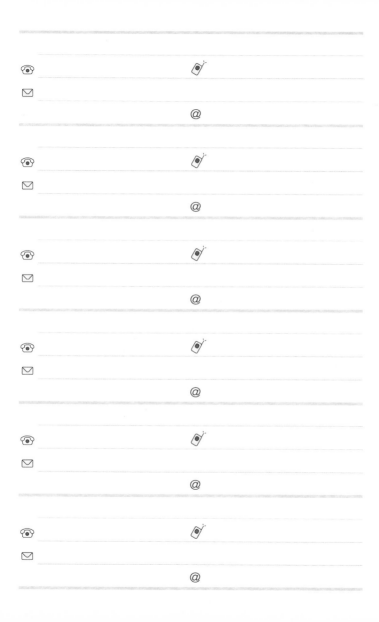

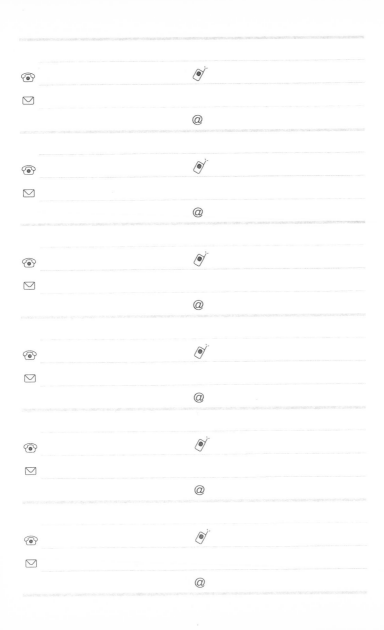

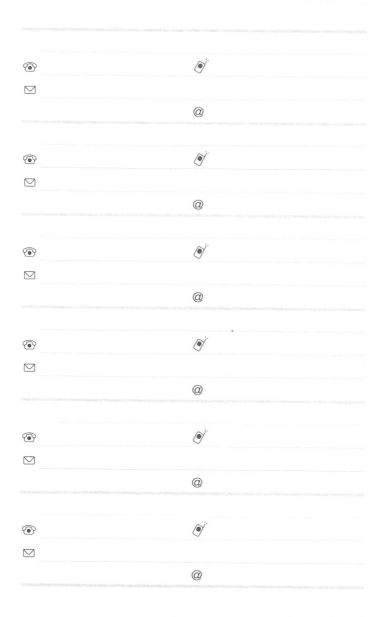

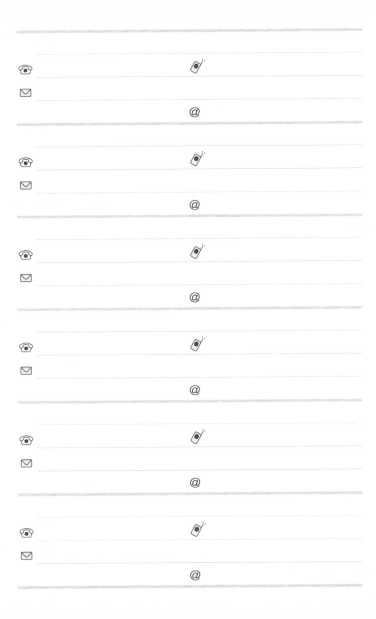

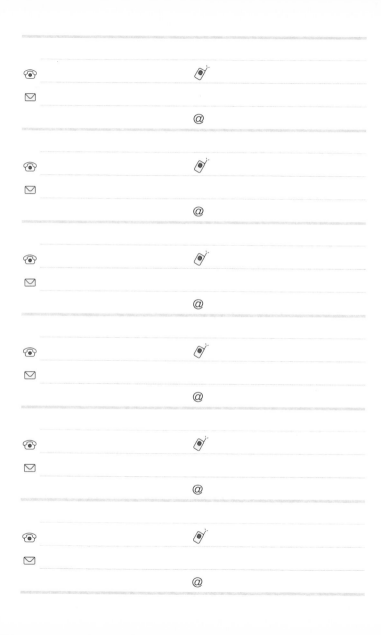

paperblanks®
FLEXI DAYPLANNERS

LINDAU

The covers of the Lindau Gospels were designed to inspire awe in early Christian onlookers when the book was carried in processions and displayed on altars. Originally tooled in gilt, silver and enamel and elaborately decorated with jewels, it is a powerful manifestation of art as a vehicle for belief.

LINDAU

Les couvertures du carnet des Évangiles de Lindau ont été conçues pour inspirer la peur chez les premiers badauds chrétiens. Le carnet était emporté lors des processions et exposé sur les autels. Originellement travaillée en dorure, argent, émail et minutieusement décorée de joyaux, elle est une puissante illustration de l'art comme vecteur de la croyance.

LINDAU

Die Bucheinbände der Lindau-Evangelien sollten bei den frühen christlichen Betrachtern ehrfürchtige Gefühle auslösen. Das Buch wurde bei Prozessionen getragen und auf den Altar gestellt. Ursprünglich mit Gold, Silber und Emaille geprägt, sowie kunstvoll mit Edelsteinen geschmückt, verdeutlicht dieser Einband eindrucksvoll wie die Kunst dem Glauben dient.

LINDAU

Le copertine dell' Evangeliario di Lindau furono ideate per incutere timore nei primi spettatori cristiani. Il libro veniva esibito durante le processioni e posto sugli altari. Originalmente impreziosito di oro, argento, smalto e laboriosamente ornato di gioielli, è una potente testimonianza dell'arte come mezzo di fede.

LINDAU

Las cubiertas de los Evangelios de Lindau fueron diseñadas para inspirar sobre-cogimiento en los primeros cristianos. Este libro se llevaba en las procesiones y se mostraba en los altares. Decorada originalmente en oro, plata y esmalte, y minuciosamente adornada con piedras preciosas, es una clara manifestación del arte como vehículo de la fe.